Amazing You

Spells

Teresa Moorey

h

a division of Hodder Headline Limited

About the series

Amazing You is our stunning new Mind Body Spirit series. It shows you how to make the most of your life and boost your chances of success and happiness. You'll discover some fantastic things about you and your friends by trying out the great tips and fun exercises. See for yourself just how amazing you can be!

Available now
Astrology
Numerology
Spells

Coming soon
Crystals
Dreams
Face and Hand Reading
Fortune Telling
Graphology
Psychic Powers

About the author

Teresa Moorey is a counsellor, astrologer and author of over forty books on witchcraft and related subjects. She is also a mother of four children aged 6–23. Teresa writes for *Mizz* magazine and *Here's Health*, and is the author of *Spell Bound: The Teenage Witch's Essential Wicca Handbook* and *Witchcraft: A Beginner's Guide*. She has written *Crystals*, *Fortune Telling* and *Graphology* in the *Amazing You* series.

Text copyright © Teresa Moorey 2004
Illustrations copyright © Jo Quinn/Inkshed 2004
Cover illustration © Monica Laita 2004

Editor: Katie Sergeant
Book design by Don Martin
Cover design: Hodder Children's Books

Published in Great Britain in 2004
by Hodder Children's Books

The right of Teresa Moorey to be identified as the author of this Work
and Jo Quinn as the illustrator of this Work has been asserted by them
in accordance with the Copyright, Designs and Patents Act 1988.

A catalogue record for this book is available from the British Library.

10 9 8 7 6 5 4 3 2 1

ISBN: 0340883669

Printed and bound by Bookmarque Ltd, Croydon, Surrey

The paper and board used in this paperback by Hodder Children's Books
are natural recyclable products made from wood grown in sustainable
forests. The manufacturing processes conform to the environmental
regulations of the country of origin.

Hodder Children's Books
a division of Hodder Headline Limited
338 Euston Road, London NW1 3BH

Contents

Introduction

Have you ever felt that you had some hidden potential, waiting to be uncovered? You are right! Do you feel you could really work magic? Right again! You are already on your way, for the first step in successful spells is belief. There are hidden powers in the human mind and you can learn to develop and focus yours for the good of yourself and others.

Working magic is like any other skill – it comes more naturally to some than to others. But anyone who really wants to can learn. The trick is to keep things simple and always to bear in mind what is in your best interests, because magic flows smoothest when it is for positive and reasonable goals.

When magic works it does so in the normal run of life – there aren't any puffs of smoke! But if you have been doing your spells well, you will know, you will feel pleased, and your powers will grow. You will also find you understand things better and that you are wiser. For instance, you will be wise enough to keep things to yourself when you need to and to realize that you do not have anything to prove. Witches have an important saying: 'Know, will, dare – and be silent!'

There are many witches around today and you have probably read about them in newspapers and magazines. In fact witchcraft is a spiritual path – the fastest growing religion among young people in Europe at the moment. Witches are Nature worshippers who care for the environment and realize that everything in the Universe is connected. When you are aware that everything is 'connected' it is natural to do spells, for these use the connections between the ordinary, everyday things that we can touch and feel and the more abstract things. A very simple example that everyone knows is that roses are associated with love. So using rose petals in a spell can help you 'plug in' to all the loving vibes around you. You will discover lots more 'connections' like this in the spells that follow.

Witches have one very strong rule: 'Harm none'. This includes you, too! All the spells in this book are 'good' spells, but you still need to think about what's best for you. For instance, would it really be a good idea to brew up a love potion if what you actually need to concentrate on is passing that maths test? Choose your spells with care!

CHAPTER ONE

Magical you

What is it that makes a true witch – or wizard?
It's basically a matter of attitude. Having an open
mind and a positive approach is important. Try
this short questionnaire to get an idea of your
current magical talents.

✴ Do you feel a strong bond with Nature or
with animals?

✴ Do your moods change with the Moon,
especially at Full Moon?

✴ Do you get 'feelings' from things like crystals
and standing stones?

✴ When you are relaxing, do you sometimes catch

a glimpse of something at the corner of your eye, but when you look there is nothing there?

✳ Have you ever dreamt about something and then it came true?

✳ Do you feel that your state of mind has an effect on what happens to you?

✳ Do you readily sense the thoughts and feelings of your friends?

✳ When you go into houses, especially old ones, are you very aware of their atmosphere?

✳ Are your first impressions about people usually correct?

✳ Do you daydream very vividly and in detail?

Count up how many 'yeses' you have answered to this quiz.

0–3 'yeses' – Even one 'yes' shows the glimmerings of magical ability, and you can build on this. If you have answered 'no' to everything, could this be because you are determined to be sceptical? In the end sceptics can make better witches, believe it or not.

4-7 'yeses' – You are on the way to developing magical awareness and talents, which are just waiting to be sharpened.

8-10 'yeses' – Impressive! Move over, Sabrina! But be careful to keep your feet on the ground, and life in perspective. ✧

Where are the witches?

There are plenty of true witches about, both men and women. They may be nurses, university lecturers or self-employed builders. Witches come from every walk of life and are very 'normal'. Witchcraft is a spiritual path of Nature worship. Doing magic arises naturally from this because witches are aware of the fact that all that exists is connected, and that everything is energy – something scientists tell us anyway. Many spells

3

can be seen as an act of worship of the beauties and gifts that Mother Nature provides.

Witches are also often called 'Wiccans', although to be exact Wicca is only one type of witchcraft. Wicca really took shape in the middle of the twentieth century, but many people believe that witchcraft is much older, even dating from the Stone Age. In 'The Craft' (as witchcraft is called) both men and women are called 'witches' – the term 'wizard' isn't used. Witches gather in groups called covens to celebrate important points in the year, such as harvest and winter solstice (i.e. Yule/Christmas). Sometimes children and young people are included in festivities, for instance at a tree-planting ceremony. However, most rituals are just for adults because witches believe it is important for young people to be able to make up their own minds about which path they are going to follow. No-one can enter a coven until they are at least 18. True witches are usually very careful indeed not to influence the young – they are aware of all the bad press that sometimes flies around! It is as well to be very careful of anyone who offers to tell you magical secrets, especially if there are any

4

strings attached, and never consent to be alone with them. As a developing witch you will realize how important your independence and safety are. Fortunately with books such as this available you do not have to rely on the whispers of anyone else – you can discover for yourself! ✧

Developing your magical senses

Being magical is a way of looking at the world – seeing through the 'ordinary' reality and glimpsing the Spirit within. But that doesn't have to be anything dramatic or overwhelming, so don't expect blinding flashes, hordes of angels or fairies. Your awareness can grow gently, and it's fun!

Magic is also about being very good at visualizing, or in some other way making your ideas real. It is about using the power of your life-force – this has been called prana, orgone, chi – all sorts of names from cultures ancient and modern. This sounds very mysterious but actually it's simple. If you think about the 'vibes' at a big football match, or the start of a party or disco you will get the feeling. It's that basic energy that is within everything – it's the 'Force' from *Star Wars*, and it's with you, in your spells.

Most spells have a part to them that 'raises power' such as a little chant, or a motion with your wand. We shall be looking at how to get your wand, among other things, in the next chapter. Witches in covens usually dance to raise power, and you can always dance before doing your spells if you wish. Maybe you feel that 'the Force is with you' anyway, and you have a sense of building up your inner power to use in your spells. Witches also use a magic circle to contain and concentrate the power they raise. We'll look at that, too, in the following chapter. In many ways your approach, awareness and attitude are the most important things. ✧

Getting tuned in

When people think about magic and the psychic arts they tend to imagine dark, candle-lit rooms, weird and mysterious symbols, robes, incense and lots of Hollywood trappings. But research has shown that the best way to develop your psychic capabilities and your intuition is simply to be in touch with nature.

You do not have to be psychic to be a witch – it isn't the same thing. There are plenty of clairvoyants who would not call themselves witches in any way shape or form, and who might well be offended by the suggestion. However, most witches have some psychic ability, or, at the least, a well-developed intuitive sense. You need this for two reasons. Firstly, good intuition will help you decide the best way to go about spells. This book gives you lots of instructions, but in the end the witch's best teacher is her instinct. Secondly, intuition helps you to 'go with the flow', getting a 'feel' for what to do, when to do it etc. It helps you to open your ears to that little voice inside that is so useful. ✧

STARTING OUT

So, for your first practical exercise, do something very simple – go for a walk! But this may well be a walk like one you have never taken before because you will be opening your eyes. Forget about spotting cute boys and don't bother to put on your best gear. Firstly be very conscious of your feet touching the ground, making contact, rising and falling in rhythm. Is the ground hard, soft or scrunchy? How does walking make you feel? Notice the sky, the shapes of clouds, the flight of birds. What colours and patterns can you see? Notice plants and flowers, the shapes of leaves, the ridges on the bark of trees. What can you smell, hear, taste? Touch things and notice the sensation.

During your walk you may pick up interesting things if you wish, as long as you are not harming the countryside or park. You may spot some unusual stones that you could use later in a spell. In autumn, you might take home an especially beautiful fallen leaf and press it between two sheets of paper. Anything that you decide to do on this walk is affirming your connection with Nature and her hidden tides of power and meaning. You don't have to try, or to work anything out. Just by being there something happens and you probably feel calmer and in a better mood.

8

During your walk, find a tree that you feel is special. Of course 'talking to trees' is a bit of a laugh, but don't let that put you off! No-one else has to know, and there is no doubt that getting in contact with trees makes people feel great! Just touch the tree's trunk, if you like. Better still, sit with your back against it. You can talk to it mentally: ask it how it feels to be out here in all winds and weathers, to have its roots deep within the earth and its branches reaching towards the sky. Ask if it will send you a special, healing force to make you feel good. Ask if it has a message for you and see if anything pops into your mind.

When you get home remember to jot down anything you have felt or seen,

and make a date to go again. Of course you will be careful not to go alone anywhere lonely or dangerous. If you can, take along a like-minded friend and the walk could be more fun. ✧

VISUALIZING

An important part of doing magic is making something real in your mind, as a prelude to making it real in the outside world. The clearer you can get this image, the better. Research on world-class athletes has shown that those who very clearly IMAGINE themselves winning are the ones that tend to come out on top. As you think, so you become!

Of course, there is more to imagining than just seeing a picture of what you want. Other senses are important, too, and different people have different senses paramount. Here is a short test to help you find out which is your strongest 'sense'.

1) Think about the last time you really enjoyed yourself. What first springs to mind?

   a) The scene, overall, as you see it.

   b) What people were saying, or the music, or sounds (such as a fountain or waves).

   c) How you were feeling inside.

2) If someone is explaining something to you, when they make themselves clear what do you tend to say?

   a) Yes, I see what you mean.

   b) I hear what you're saying and it sounds fine.

   c) That's sunk in – I understand.

3) Think about your most vivid childhood memory. Does it come back to you as

   a) A picture?

   b) A sound?

   c) An emotion or sensation?

If you answered 'as' then your most easily
accessed faculty is vision, if 'bs' then it is hearing,
if 'cs' then you are more focused on your inward
feelings. Of course, this is a great simplification,
because the human mind is very complex. This is
just to help you to be aware that there are
different ways of perceiving and processing
information.

People whose strongest sense is visual have
something of an advantage in certain respects,
because it is often easier to take in a lot, visually.
This applies when you are revising for exams; the
visual types can remember more information by
looking at a school book. Others need to hear to
remember but they may not realize this and may
think they're 'thick' until they discover that by
recording information on a tape and playing it, it
sinks in. Those who are more 'into' their
sensations may be artistic, creative, good at drama
or dance – there are many possibilities.

Firstly, let's practise visualizing. Sit yourself
comfortably and quietly, and close your eyes.
Imagine that you are in a cinema. In front of you
there is a big, blank screen. Now think of
somewhere that you would like to be – preferably

somewhere that is fresh in your mind, so you can 'see' every detail – somewhere like the beach, or a disco. Look at the imaginary screen and 'see' the scene appearing on it. Watch it, examine it, let your eyes travel over it. Let it take on a life of its own, watch it unfolding, observe what happens. Now make something happen. See this taking place in as much detail as you can. You are in control, you decide what appears on your screen.

Do this for as long as feels comfortable. Then turn off your screen – run some credits if you like. Let the screen go blank and come back to everyday awareness. Pat yourself all over and get grounded by having a sip of water. You can practise this every day, for five minutes or so, and when you feel confident you can start visualizing things you want to happen in your life, as a first bit of magic.

What to do if you can't visualize? Can you imagine hearing? Close your eyes and imagine you are listening to the radio. Choose what you want to hear and imagine it coming to your ears clearly and audibly. Or imagine a friend phoning you with just the news that you want, talking about exactly what has happened.

If you are more 'into' your feelings, sit quietly and imagine that a certain emotion or sensation is filling you – always choose something pleasant, of course! Things that you have recently felt will be more vivid. When you are ready, progress to what you would like to feel.

The point is to find a way in to your ability to 'make real' inside your head. If you feel you really aren't imaginative at all (and this will probably be because you are letting yourself get uptight) don't worry! When you are doing magic you can use any little props or reminders that you might need, such as pictures, to get your mind in gear. ✧

A word on relaxing

It isn't always easy to let yourself go all floppy, but it is important in magic because if you're tense it gets in the way of the subtle psychic tides and isolates you. Obviously when you are doing spells you won't be lying down with your eyes closed, but still a habit of being relaxed and loose makes things flow more easily.

 Essential oil of lavender, easily obtained in most health food stores at about £5 a bottle, is very useful for many spells and is especially good to help you unwind. Place just a little on your wrist or temple. This is a very gentle oil but allergies are still possible so test first by a tiny drop on your wrist alone and wait for 24 hours before further use.

Settle yourself and imagine that you are under a warm shower. Feel the gentle drops on your head, face and body. Feel the warmth flowing over you, starting at the top of your head, going down over your neck, shoulders, arms, hands and

fingers, and now down your chest
and back, stomach and pelvis. Aaah!
All the tension is being washed away,
leaving only blissful relaxation. Now
this lovely feeling is spreading down your legs,
knees, calves, ankles, heels, feet and finally
through your toes leaving your body wonderfully
relaxed and stress-free. Ready to get magical? ✧

Being one of the good guys

When you do magic you are reaching out into the
realms of the unseen. Some people talk about the
'dangers' of the occult. The truth of the matter is
that you are in far, far more danger riding your
bike along a busy road than you will ever be
doing a spell. However, it is very important to go
about things in the right way, whatever you are
doing in life, and especially so in magic.

The first, and most important thing to
remember is that no magic should ever be
designed to affect the life path of another person.

This means, for instance, that any love spell must be about attracting general love, or a type of person, but never at one specific person. To ignore this is to ask for trouble. A general love spell is like putting up a roadside advert to all the passing cars (i.e. potential partners) saying, 'I'm here, this is what I want and I'm gonna get it. Is it you? Are you game?' The right 'car' for you will then turn off the road and find you, safely. But trying to stop one specific car could be like jumping out in front of it. You'll get their attention but you could cause a mega accident.

It is far, far better to keep spells general, for they are no less effective and that way the Universe is hot-wired to give you what is best for you – which may actually be a lot better than what you think you want. The rule of not targeting anyone directly even applies to things like bullying. Yes, you are quite within your rights to protect yourself from bullies, but what you are working on is that person's behaviour towards you, or your friends, not themselves. They do not have a right to hurt you or anyone else, but it is not up to you to try to get your own back magically. The witches' golden rule is **'Harm none'**.

This brings us to another important point: all you do comes back to you in some form or another. Always remember that, whatever spells you decide on. Think clearly about what you set in motion – it's like a boomerang. Are you happy for it to return to sender?

Finally, witches work for the good of the earth. In later chapters we shall be looking at some spells you can do for the environment. So much harm is being done to the earth and there is strife and pollution all around the globe. A little magic goes a long way when it comes to sending out some good vibes to compensate, and you'll feel great for doing it! ✧

CHAPTER TWO

Getting the gear

Spells are a way of 'spelling out' what you want so that it sinks deep into your subconscious and makes a big statement in the unseen realms. What you use in spells is symbolic. Although all the spells in this book are simple, they are based on some very old associations.

It's a good idea to have some basic equipment when you start doing spells. It's more fun that way, and it works better because when you have things by you that you've chosen especially for your magic you feel great, and it gets you in the mood just by looking and touching. Anyway, a basic spell-kit makes sense as there are many things you'll use again and again. The spells in this book use very limited ingredients to make it easy and cheap, but you can branch out later with some ideas from the appendix on p109 if you like.

Chalice ★★

A chalice is just a special glass with a
stem. It's especially sacred to the
Mother Goddess because it's shaped
like a womb, and so perfect for your
magical potions. Look round charity shops for
something that takes your eye. Wash it out with
salt and spring water saying three times:

For my magic you I choose
Be clean and safe for me to use.

NB Avoid silver plating or any surface that might
tarnish, taint or peel off.

Candles ★★

Buy these in as many colours as you like
and make sure you have very solid candle-
holders for them. Candles are used a great
deal in magic but you have to be very
careful with them. NEVER leave them
unattended and make sure they are well away
from clothes, curtains and your hair! If your folks

ban candles, ask if they would let you have a lantern instead, so the flame is protected. If they still say no, try using a torch with coloured tissue paper over the bulb. Be careful the torch doesn't get too hot.

Joss sticks and holders ✴✴

Joss sticks are really a type of incense and you can find a wide selection in New Age shops. Because these are less of a fire hazard than candles, your folks are less likely to object to them, but you will still need to be sure that you have a proper joss stick holder that keeps the stick steady and catches the ash. Choose one that makes you feel magical if you like, such as a dragon-shaped dish or one with a crystal set within. Again, New Age and gift shops have a wide selection. Joss sticks don't cost much per packet. Leaf through a few of the spells in this book and get some packets in advance, according to what you think you'll need.

21

Stone ★★

This won't cost you anything! On one of your walks look out for a stone with an appealing shape or colour and take it home with you. Hold it in your hand when you are feeling peaceful, and think loving thoughts. Avoid touching it when you are tense. It is your link with Mother Earth, and you can have it near you when you are doing your spells to increase your power.

If you look at the first four pieces of kit you will see that they represent the Four Elements that ancient people believed formed the basis of the universe: Earth (stone), Fire (candle), Air (joss stick), and Water (chalice). This is still true today for all substances are either solid, liquid, gas or burning. These four Elements are very magical to witches.

Wand ★★

From Merlin to Harry Potter every wizard has a wand. The staff carried by Gandalf, in *The Lord of the Rings*, is an essential conductor of his power. A wand helps you to focus your energy, to use your imagination creatively and positively. Lots of the spells in the following pages will involve your wand. Real witches today use wands in their rites.

Your wand, again, is something that need cost you nothing (although if you have lots of Christmas or birthday money you could splash out on something flashy, with a crystal at the tip). Truly, however, the best wand is one you make yourself. You can do this by looking for a piece of fallen wood or finding a friendly tree and asking it, mentally, if it minds you taking some of its wood. If you feel the answer is yes, cut the wood carefully. Don't damage the tree, or upset the neighbours by attacking their ornamental cherry tree! Cut your wand the length of your forearm and rub some olive oil into it, to keep the wood supple, and the job is done! You may also attach a small crystal or an acorn to the end if you wish but make sure you don't use anything toxic in case your wand touches your potions.

Traditionally, different woods have different

powers and you may like to choose accordingly, or have several wands. Here is a selection of woods and their meanings:

WILLOW – dreams, healing, psychism

HAZEL – inspiration, mental clarity

OAK – power, authority, good fortune

APPLE – love, Mother Goddess, the power of Nature

YEW – wisdom, immortality, visions

BLACKTHORN – authority

ASH – protection, versatility, revelation

BIRCH – purification, new life

BEECH – creativity

BAY – inspiration, prophecy, good fortune

ELDER – clairvoyance, peace, Grandmother Goddess

PINE – energy, protection, cleansing.

If you want to choose your wand according to the wood, go for something that feels 'right' for you. Whatever wood your wand is made of, you may use it for any magic you do.

Essential oils ★★

These are often used in spells and
cost about £5 a bottle. Store them
carefully, away from the light and
take care what surfaces they touch

for they may stain. Lavender is very handy, multi-
purpose and very mild. It is used in lots of spells.

Crystals ★★

Small 'tumblestones' may be £1 each and are very
useful as charms and gifts for 'good luck'. Some
of the spells include semi-precious stones. You
can either buy them when you need
them or look out for cheap ones to
stock up. Rose quartz, crystal and
amber may all be useful. Holey
stones, which are simply small stones with
naturally occurring holes, are very lucky and
sacred to the Mother Goddess. You may even find
some on the beach. Doughnut stones from New
Age shops are a good substitute.

25

Robe ★★

If you want to get togged up for your spells, a robe makes you feel really magical. Any long garment will do as long as it's a colour that feels right. Dark blue, brown or purple may be better than black. Look out for something suitable (and washable) in a charity shop, soak it in salt water for 24 hours, and say the same words given for cleansing your chalice (see page 20). Then wash it in the usual way with the rest of your clothes.

Notebook and pen ★★

Last but not least, you will need something to make notes about spells you have done, how you have felt, what has happened, etc.

MAGIC CIRCLE PROTECTION SPELL

Now you have all your stuff, for your first bit of magic you can make a magic circle. Witches use this for their rites. They believe it makes a secure place to do spells – a place that is half in the spirit world, half in this world. Making your magic circle is great practice in protecting yourself, too.

Find out which part of your room faces North and put the stone there. Put a white or red candle or torch in the South, a joss stick in the East and your chalice in the West. These are the traditional places for the Four Elements, although if you live in the Southern Hemisphere it is better to have your stone in the South, candle in North. This is because in the Southern Hemisphere the Sun is in the North of the sky so North is best linked to fire and South with Earth and darkness. In the Southern Hemisphere the Sun moves anti-clockwise too.

Sit in the middle of your magical objects and imagine there is a circle around you. Draw this with your wand if you like (clockwise in the Northern Hemisphere, anti-clockwise in the Southern). Remember your cinema visualization (see pages 12–13)? Imagine you are now on the screen, in the story, and create your circle in whatever way is best for you. See it, hear it humming like a power-line, feel it vibrating. Feel quite relaxed and continue visualizing the circle so that it feels really strong. Make it into a big bubble that goes all round you. When you are ready to stop, imagine pulling the circle back inside you, so you re-absorb the energy.

When you are good at making your circle you can do it quickly when you want to feel secure – you can do it just by visualizing, without your equipment. You can also put it round you when doing your spells, but remember to send the spell strongly out of the circle and always re-absorb the energies of your circle or you could feel 'funny'.

Now you have done your first bit of magic, it is time to move on to some spells ... ✧

CHAPTER THREE

All loved up

Love spells are the best of all. You feel fab when you're doing them and even better when they work! Just remember the golden rule about not influencing any specific person and everything will be fine. ✧

MAKING A ROSE QUARTZ CHARM

You will need
* Venus statue/picture
* rose quartz
* rose or jasmine joss stick
* fresh or dried rose petals
* two deep pink candles
* a dish
* sweets or chocolates

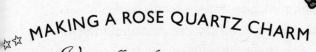

NB If you can't get a Venus picture, choose one that reminds you of the Love Goddess. Rose quartz is a happy and gentle stone and you'll feel good just by touching it. If you can find it in a pendant you'll be able to wear it later, if not just carry it in your bag. Choose a piece of rose quartz that makes you feel good when you touch it.

Light two deep pink candles. Place your rose petals in a pink dish, or better still a heart-shaped one, and put the rose quartz in the centre of the petals. Burn the joss stick. If you have a statue of Venus make sure she is there to watch over you. Close your eyes and imagine the Goddess of Love commanding anything that is negative to leave the room.

Hold your hands, palms open, over the rose petals, and imagine love, warmth and attractiveness going into the petals and the quartz. Say three times:

Magic stone, draw to me
All love that's mine, rightfully.

Imagine yourself feeling blissfully loved, having just the right person for you fancying you like mad! Imagine all the fun you'll have. Imagine

30

holding hands, talking, laughing (careful now –
don't think about people you know!). Smile to
yourself just thinking about all the good things
coming your way.

Now move your candles until they are close
together. Eat your sweets or chocolates. Place
your rose quartz somewhere safe and end your
spell by putting out your candles. You can re-light
them, if you like, whenever you are getting ready
to go out somewhere special, to re-enforce your
charm. Wear, or take your rose quartz with you
and wait for the honey-bees to swarm! ✧

MAKING A ROSE PETAL CHARM

This sizzling sachet will surround you with loving
vibes. Make it when the Moon is full if you can
and romance is in the bag!

You will need ✳ your stone
✳ dried rose petals
✳ a circle of pink cloth, about 12cm
in diameter, or square

31

* matching thread and/or ribbon
* lavender oil or your favourite perfume
* deep pink candles
* rose or jasmine joss stick

Light the candles and the joss stick. Sit quietly and imagine the kind of person you would like to meet. Mentally list all the things that are most important to you.

Hold a small clump of rose petals between your hands and imagine that you are pouring

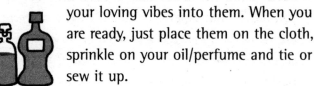 your loving vibes into them. When you are ready, just place them on the cloth, sprinkle on your oil/perfume and tie or sew it up.

To bring yourself back to earth, place your palms on your stone and ask the Great Mother to make your spell real. Snuff out your candles. Keep your sachet with you whenever you are out on the prowl! As in the Rose Quartz Charm spell, you can re-light your candles for extra oomph before any special date. ✧

AMAZING APHRODITE

The Greek goddess Aphrodite is still the coolest goddess around. She's at home in any disco or party, but her favourite haunts are the wild places in nature, for she, like love, can never be tamed. Try this visualization to get in her groove.

Light a joss stick – rose or ylang-ylang are good – and sit quietly and peacefully. Imagine you are in that cinema, in front of the big screen, and what you can see is a wonderful woodland scene, full of wild deer, waterfalls and flowering bushes. Now climb into the screen, into the virtual world of greenery that is now your world.

Find yourself following a winding path that is going deeper and deeper into the heart of the forest. The light is becoming dimmer, but around you there rises a wonderful and exotic scent. Walk along the tangled path for a while, noticing what is around you.

Now you come into a small clearing. Beside it there is a small lake whose waters are clear

 emerald. Ahead of you there is a tunnel, made of roses. Now you realize that the scent you have been following has come from these amazing flowers whose heady fragrance almost makes you dizzy.

You now go through the rose tunnel. It twists and turns so you cannot see where you are going, but all around you there is a pink glow. Now you come out of the tunnel into an open space. The grass beneath your feet is springy, and ahead, on a lush bank, the goddess Aphrodite sits with her attendants around her.

What does she say to you? What do you ask her? What do you learn? Stay with her as long as you like. If she gives you a gift, treasure it. Thank her for her time. When you are ready make your way back, not by the rose tunnel but by a route that opens alongside it.

Go back along the forest path and find yourself out in your cinema again. Sit and watch the screen go blank. If you were given a gift, imagine yourself putting it in a safe at the back of the cinema. Open your eyes and come back to everyday awareness. Eat a chocolate or sweet to ground yourself and say a big thank you to Aphrodite. If you feel you have learnt anything important be sure to jot it down. ✧

✩✩ BATHING BEAUTY

For some extra oomph before a very special occasion, try this magical hot-tub.

You will need
* rose petals (dried ones will be fine)
* deep pink candles
* lavender essence/pure essential oil
* a dish

If you have not already done so, test the lavender essence 24 hours beforehand, on the inside of your wrist, to make sure you aren't allergic to it.

Light some deep pink candles in the bathroom making sure the flames are reflected in the water.

Drop five drops of lavender essence in the bathwater and sprinkle on some dried rose petals.

As you immerse yourself in the water, imagine the warmth going deep inside you, making you radiant and irresistible.

Soak in the water, gently picking out the rose petals in pairs and putting them in the dish. As you squeeze them together repeat over and over again:

Two as one together shall be
He with me, me with he.

If there is an uneven number of petals, just fold the last one in two and say the rhyme. Keep all the petals together in the dish. Get ready in your usual way, but as you go take the dish to the door with you and throw the damp rose petals on your path. Go, go, GO! (Make sure you tidy up after yourself – this will help you 'close down', and bring you back to normal life again.) ✧

☆☆ FEELING FRUITY

Apples have lots of magical meanings. The Celts believed they were the fruit of the gods.

You will need
* one apple
* a knife to cut the apple
* a stream

First hold your apple and imagine the kind of love you want. Cut your apple in half, cross-wise. If you look you can see the core appears like a five-pointed star, or pentagram. Witches believe this is sacred to the Mother Goddess. Eat one half of the apple and take the other half to the stream. Let it float downstream, saying:

> *I cast my wish upon the tide*
> *Waters, bring love to my side.*

... and just go with the flow! ◇

37

☆☆ MELTING MOMENTS

Melt the heart of a lush lad with this sweet spell.

You will need   * a warm drink
                  * a sugar cube

Hold the sugar cube in the palm of your left
hand, close your eyes and think of the kind of
boy you would like to meet (be reasonable – no
pop stars!). Imagine a stream of light going down
your arm and into the cube. When you are ready,
transfer the cube to your right hand and say:

Sugar, sugar, oh so sweet
Now this boy and I will meet
Sugar, sugar, play your part
As you melt, so melt his heart.

Drop the sugar cube into the drink, let it melt
and drink up! ✧

38

CHAPTER FOUR

Beautiful you

You are beautiful as the Goddess made you - it's true! Of course that's hard to believe when you've got a huge spot and it's a bad hair day! When that happens try not to dwell on it. Don't look at yourself in the mirror and say, 'I'm a disaster', just dismiss it as what it is – a mood – and do something nice to cheer yourself up. Never try to conform to stereotypes – it's boring! Surveys show that tastes vary enormously; all shapes and sizes are found beautiful by somebody. What matters most is being fun to be with, and that comes from loving yourself and accepting yourself. Spells can help boost your self-esteem, and then you can use them to get some great clobber and magical skin care. ✧

★ ✳ ★

TRUE BEAUTY

Use this spell to put you in touch with your own, individual beauty.

You will need
* an orange or gold candle
* a piece of amber (or orange stone or gold jewellery)
* a gold/orange coloured nightie (a cheap large T-shirt will be fine)
* a mirror
* bubble bath

Do this spell at the end of the day, when you are ready to relax and go to bed. Light your candle in the bathroom and make sure that the flame is reflected in the bubbles. Run your bath with plenty of bubbles for you to enjoy. Get into the bath and relax, taking your piece of amber with you. Gently run the amber stone (or piece of gold) over your body, as you relax, watching the bubbles and dancing flames.

40

When you are ready, get out, towel off and put on your nightie. Turn off any lights so that you are seeing by candlelight. Hold your amber (or gold) between your palms and look into the mirror. Make sure that the glow of the candle is falling on your face. Look deep into your eyes and say, 'I am beautiful. My beauty shines from within. I love my body.' Repeat this as many times as you like, but at least three times. Place the amber (or gold) under your pillow. Repeat this spell as necessary. ✧

☆☆ ZAP THE ZIT

Isn't it the pits when you have a spot right in the middle of your face, especially before a special date? This spell will help get rid of it.

You will need
* a piece of clear crystal
* some tea-tree oil
* salt and water

NB Make sure the tea-tree oil is diluted because pure tea tree may be too harsh. Body Shop make a diluted version, or use tea-tree cream. Also be sure to test the tea-tree oil on your wrist 24 hours beforehand to test for any allergies.

Cleanse your crystal by leaving it overnight in water in which you have dissolved a pinch of salt. When you apply your tea-tree lotion, squeeze or drop it first on to the crystal, and from there on to your spot. Re-cleanse your crystal regularly. It is also a good idea to point an angle of your crystal towards your spot, imagining a clear stream of purifying light zapping the zit like a laser. You can also lie in bed at night imagining a green light focused on the zit, shrinking it and taking away the inflammation. ✧

✩✩ GROOVY GEAR

You know you look the biz – all you need is that fab frock or cool new boots to complete your outfit. Try this spell before hitting the high street, so the clothes leap off the rails at you!

You will need
* your wand
* your stone
* a picture or drawing of the clothes you want
* a magnet
* some dried sage

Your Mum or Dad will probably have some dried sage in the kitchen. However, if you have some fresh sage growing in a pot or in the garden, take a leaf of that instead. Now sit peacefully and comfortably and look at your picture/s. Really imagine that the clothes you want are yours. See them hanging in your cupboard. See yourself wearing them, feeling great. Take up your magnet and place it on top of the picture of your clothes and tap it with your wand.

Wrap the sage up in the picture. If you are just about to go shopping, place it in your cupboard with your stone. If your planned shopping trip is for another day, sleep with it under your pillow. When you go shopping take your magnet with you. Retail therapy here we come! ✧

43

CONJURING CASH

Money to spend on new clothes and make-up makes you feel great. If your funds need a boost from the subtle realms, try this spell. It really is best performed when the Moon is waxing (growing from new to full), so take a peek at the paper – the phases are usually shown somewhere.

You will need
* a green candle
* a small green bag or purse
* your wand
* some grains of rice on a green dish, if possible
* a pound coin
* your stone

Light your candle and place your pound coin in the centre of the dish of rice. Say three times:

Sky above and earth below
See my money grow and grow.

Tap the gold coin with your wand. Sit quietly imagining the money that you need coming to you in normal ways. Be very clear about the amount you need and keep it sensible. Imagine yourself having opportunities to earn money. Visualize yourself having it and spending it, and how you will feel.

When you have envisaged all you can put the pound coin into the purse along with most of the rice. Keep a little of the rice to scatter outside. Sleep with the purse under your pillow, or place it with your stone until your money comes. ✧

☆☆ SELF-ESTEEM SPELL

Self-esteem comes from feeling okay inside, that we are special in our own right without having to copy anyone else or measure up to anyone else's standards. It's an inner glow.

For this spell you'll have to put in a bit of work researching goddesses because there isn't room to describe them much here. You could try the Internet or my book, *The Goddess a Beginner's Guide*, published by Hodder Mobius. Here is a quick run-through of some of the better known goddesses.

VENUS – beauty, harmony, attractiveness, symbol an apple

ATHENE – wisdom, justice, symbol an owl

ISIS – total goddess-power, symbol a throne

ARTEMIS – independence, girl-power, symbol a wild deer

RHIANNON – mystery, exploration, symbol a horse

SEKHMET – very powerful, strong and energetic, symbol a lion.

Choose a goddess that is special to you and find out all you can about her. Get yourself something that represents her, such as a stone or her symbol.

Read about her, think about her, until you feel
you really know her. Find a statue or picture that
looks like you think she does, if you can.

When you are alone think about your goddess.
Ask her to give you her power, to make you feel
good deep inside, to shine. Think about her as
your friend, but a very powerful one indeed. Get
something that symbolizes her, light a candle,
hold the symbol in your hand and ask your
goddess to put her power into the symbol for
you. Say:

> *Goddess, be within me at all times and make*
> *me shine.*
> *Blessed Be.*

Fill your chalice with your favourite fruit juice and
toast her health at every Full Moon. Now you
have all the help you need. ✧

CHAPTER FIVE

Magical mates

It's fun to do magic with your mates – it brings you closer. However, you need to be careful who you do your magic with. Only do it with friends that you really trust, and don't get too intense. There's nothing more magical than a giggle, anyway! ✧

✩✩ FRIENDSHIP SCROLL

This is a spell to do with a group of friends, and is great for a sleepover. It is intended to give everyone confidence that they are liked and accepted. You can do it with just one friend, but it doesn't work quite so well. It is essential that everyone taking part in this spell really likes everyone else and wants to make it work. Make sure everyone properly understands and wants to take part before you get going.

You will need
* a soft pink candle
* a sheet of pink paper
* some pink ribbon
* a pen each
* some lavender oil

Light the candle and sit round it in a circle, each

of you with your sheet of paper in front of you. Put your name at the top of the paper, and if you've got a nice sticker, like a star or a rainbow to decorate it with, add that too.

Now each of you passes the paper to the person on the left. That person writes their name below yours along with something they really like or admire about you. It could be something they think you're really good at, something you did really well or anything that is REALLY NICE. Continue passing the papers round, writing your name and comment until everyone has written on everyone's page and the pages are back with their original owners.

Now each person can look at their sheet. Chances are you'll be delighted and surprised! Talk about it for a while if you like. Now everyone should put a drop of lavender oil on all four corners of their paper and roll it up, tying it with the ribbon. Keep your special scroll safe and re-read it to get that inner glow. ✧

✩✩ LOVING CUP

This is a quick spell to do with one or more VERY close friends, or that special boy.

You will need
* your chalice
* red grape juice
* runny honey
* your wand

Fill your chalice with red grape juice and add just a little runny honey. Hold your wand over it, think warm and loving thoughts and imagine a stream of light going into the liquid from your wand. Say out loud:

By the cycles of Moon and Sun
Always we two shall be as one.

Take it in turns to hold the chalice so the other may drink. This spell will bind you psychically, but it will not mean that either owns the other or that no-one can change. It is about respect, caring and honesty – who could ask for more? ✧

☆☆ TEXT SPELL

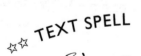 *You will need* ✳ your mobile
　　　　　　　　　　 ✳ some magical intentions!

Just text in the usual way, but have a clear idea of a feeling that you would especially like to send, such as love, sympathy, cheer up or stay cool. If you're texting that lad and you want to play it cool, you might send a funny text but want to send an unwritten message like, 'Cor – tell me you fancy me!'

Focus on one word in the text that you want to take your message and spell this one out properly. Words like 'great', 'fabulous' and 'wonderful' are good examples. Stare at the word and think clearly of your unspoken message. Say it over and over again.

As you press 'send' imagine your thoughts going towards the person like a beam of white light. Imagine how they look when they receive the message and imagine getting a great message back. Beep, beep, beep, beep! ✧

HARMONY IN THE GANG

Everyone snarling? Don't stress. Try this quick spell to bring you all closer.

You will need   ✳ one orange
                  ✳ your wand

When you are alone, just think of peace and harmony between all your friends. Then tap the orange six times with your wand. Pull it into segments and share it with your friends. Sorted! ✧

☆☆ MAKING NEW FRIENDS

Not got enough mates at the moment? This spell will increase your circle of friends.

You will need
* ✳ a pink garment (this can be underwear, if you like)
* ✳ some pink paper
* ✳ a pen
* ✳ scissors
* ✳ some rose oil (or perfume)
* ✳ your stone
* ✳ your wand

Cut out a heart shape from the paper. Write on the paper:

Friends for me
So shall it be.

Put a little of the oil on to the heart-shaped paper and some on to your garment (it may stain, so put it somewhere that doesn't show). Visualize lots of cool new friends, or one special one. Make sure you focus on general people, not someone in particular. Wrap the heart in your garment and leave them together overnight, with your stone.

The next day, place the heart in the corner of your bedroom that is to the right and nearest you when you walk in through the door. Wear the garment and go out smiling. When your garment goes in the wash you can re-charge it by wrapping it up overnight with the heart again. ✧

☆☆ MEAN MATE RECOVERY

If a mate has been mean to you the chances are you feel pretty down for a while. This spell will help you recover and smile again.

You will need ✳ a small white candle
✳ some lavender oil

Rub a few drops of the oil into the candle before you light it, saying as often as you like:

Mean friend, no friend
My heart shall mend.

Light the candle and relax. Let the hurt roll off you. Let the candle burn for a while (but don't leave it unattended). Soon you will feel much better and as if a weight has been lifted off your shoulders. ✧

✫✫ FRIENDSHIP BRACELET

If you have a special friend you may want to forge a strong bond between you. Try this spell to cement your friendship.

You will need ✳ three lengths of cord (silk thread)
✳ some apple juice
✳ your chalice

56

Both of you should choose one length of cord in your favourite colour, while the third should be yellow because it is cheerful and indicates good communication.

Clasp hands with your friend, holding the three cords between your palms. Say together:

Friends forever
Honest and true
You care for me
And I care for you!

Now cut the cords in half and plait them. When you have finished, swap plaits and tie the bracelet round your wrist. Share some apple juice in your chalice. ✧

✩✩ FABULOUS FACE PACK

When you've got all the gang together for a sleepover, why not make your own yummy face pack, from all natural ingredients, and give each other a beauty bonanza?

You will need ✳ four soft strawberries
✳ a tablespoon of thick Greek yoghurt
✳ one tablespoon of honey

You will need a helping of all of these for each person taking part. NB It is important that you test anything you put on your skin for allergies first, even if it is a totally natural substance. Do this by putting a little on the inside of your wrist 24 hours before use.

Strawberries are ruled by Venus, goddess of beauty, and yoghurt is ruled by the Moon, linked to feminine rhythms. So here you have the two Ladies of the Sky on side, with some extra oomph from sunny honey.

Mash up the strawberries in a roomy dish, using a fork. Then stir in the honey and yoghurt. Say:

Goddess, shining up above
Give us your beauty, with your love.

If all your sleepover friends are 'into' magic then circle the mixture with your wand a few times. Now take it in turns to smooth the mixture gently

58

over each others' faces, repeating the rhyme if you like. After five minutes, gently wash off the mixture with cold water and cotton wool and pat dry. What a lot of Sleeping Beauties! ✧

✦✦✦
Elementary, my dear!

We met the Elements in Chapter Two (see page 22). They have links with our abilities and gifts and they are deeply magical. Each sign of the zodiac belongs to one of the Elements: Aries, Leo and Sagittarius are Fire; Taurus, Virgo and Capricorn are Earth; Gemini, Libra and Aquarius are Air; and Cancer, Scorpio and Pisces are Water.

It sometimes helps to get an extra helping of an Element. If you are a Fire or Air sign, some Water or Earth may help balance you. If you are an Earth or Water sign try Air and Fire. Besides this, there are times when we could all do with a bit of one Element or the other for an extra magical boost.

If you are feeling sluggish, can't think clearly, can't manage to talk things through or get anything sorted, or if you have lots of schoolwork and exams, you need some AIR! Things to do: go and fly a kite, go bird-watching, take a walk to the top of a windy hill, blow bubbles, play with balloons.

If you're getting fed up with each other, haven't much sympathy for each others' moans, are losing that feeling of closeness and support you need some WATER! Things to do: go swimming together, have a hand-washing party with some olive soap and hand cream, sit by a lake and have a heart-to-heart, make each other a yummy drink, have a foot party and soak your feet together using lemon scrub and lemon lotion, share a bunch of white grapes. Chop up a cucumber and each of you close your eyes and lie down with a slice on each eye for ten minutes – you'll feel chilled and totally chummy.

If you're a bit spaced out, spending too much money, forgetting everything, being scatty, losing stuff, you're often late and can't seem to finish things, then you need a dose of EARTH! Things to do: plant seeds, help out in the garden, plant a tree, re-pot a house plant, make a great big cake full of dried fruit, or have a competition to see who can collect the most unusual stone when you're out on a walk.

If you're feeling bored, you can't get ideas for a creative project, you're lacking energy and zest for life or you're feeling a bit down and negative, you need the gift of FIRE! Fire is a tricky Element – that's why we all love it! Don't take chances with it though. Things to do: light a candle and sit round it and 'brainstorm', let off some fireworks (always follow instructions and get an adult to help), if you are lucky enough to have an open fire look for pictures in the molten caverns in the coal, have a bonfire (again, this depends on the adults).

The world is full of magical meanings – let them in! ✧

☆☆ SLEEPOVER SPELL

Lots of the previous spells are good for sleepovers. Here is one to give you all sweet dreams. It is based on the Native American idea of dream catchers, which catch the bad dreams and let only good dreams in.

You will need
* a lacy scarf or piece of lace
* two feathers
* a five-point star symbol
* a Moon symbol
* a symbol for each person at the sleepover

The scarf or lace should be black, white, deep blue, purple or grey. See if your mum has got one she doesn't wear. Thread or sew the feathers to opposite ends of the scarf or lace and fix the star and Moon on to it. Each person should sew or stick their symbol on the lace, very securely. If you are not sure what symbols to choose, just an initial would do, a symbol of your astrological sign or an animal that you feel is special to you.

When you have finished your dream catcher ask for it to be blessed by the Great Mother and for you all to have really special dreams. Hang the dream catcher in the window. Next morning be sure to tell each other about your amazing dreams. Why not write them down? ✧

CHAPTER SIX

School's cool

Don't worry, whatever they say your schooldays are NOT the best days of your life. Better things are coming, trust me! However, you can have a fab time at school if you think positively and act sensibly – and grab yourself a little help from the subtle realms! ✧

✩✩ CLASSROOM CONFIDENCE

It can be very scary if you're starting at a new school where you don't know anybody, or if you have to stand up in front of the class to do or say something. Don't worry, you are not alone!

Almost everyone feels that way – they just hide it, like you probably do. Doing a spell beforehand will help you face any situation with more confidence.

You will need
* a gold candle
* a length of golden wool or thin cord
* three sunflower seeds (on a gold dish if possible)
* your wand

Light your candle and sit quietly thinking about three things that would make things go well for you. For instance you might think that being calm, looking your best and remembering everything would help. Perhaps you can only think of one thing – that doesn't matter. Tap each of the sunflower seeds in turn, saying aloud one of the things you want, as if you are naming them. Or say the same thing three times.

Take up your cord and tie a knot in it for each of your intentions, saying:

For [first intention] I tie knot Number One
Now my spell is sure begun

For [second intention] I tie knot Two
My spell is growing strong and true
For [third intention] I fix knot Three
Now this thing shall really be.

Fasten the cord around your wrist and eat the sunflower seeds. Wear the wristlet whenever you are facing challenging situations – it will give you strength and assurance. ✧

☆☆ BANISHING BULLYING

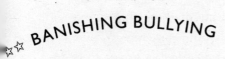

Bullying is a horrible thing and you don't have to put up with it. Firstly, if you are bullied the first thing you must do is tell a responsible adult, and make sure they take notice of the fact that this is serious.

It may be hard to believe that bullies are really weak people – but they are! People who don't really feel likeable and acceptable sometimes make themselves feel better by making others feel like outcasts. People who have no real inner strength get an illusion of power by making others feel scared. One of the reasons bullies are so good at getting under your skin and making you feel afraid and vulnerable is because they know all the weak spots – they've got them too!

Because bullying is such an important issue, we have two powerful spells for it. First up ...

☆☆ DISSOLVE THE DREAD SPELL
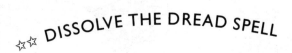

You will need
* a soluble dark brown stock cube preferably in a flavour you dislike
* some hot water
* an old mug (don't use your chalice)

Take hold of the stock cube and project all your fear and unpleasant feelings into it. You don't want these feelings, you don't want this situation – it is all ugly and dark like the brown cube. These feelings are going. Affirm that to yourself.

66

Drop the cube into the mug and carefully pour hot water on to it. See it melt, all its substance dissolving so that it is just brown sludge. Make sure it has thoroughly dissolved.

Now pour the nasty mixture down the toilet or outside on to the ground. Repeat this as often as you like until the feelings are gone. ✧

Our second spell is ...

✩✩ BIND THE BULLY

It's important that you do this right. Remember that you are not supposed to harm anyone – this spell is to stop this person from hurting you. You have a perfect right to protect yourself, but not to ill-wish.

You will need   ✳ a sheet of white paper
                  ✳ a black pen
                  ✳ some black wool
                  ✳ a black candle
                  ✳ your wand

Light your candle and sit in front of it, feeling relaxed. The Mother Goddess is with you – let this

thought fuel your determination to stop the bullying. When you feel ready, write the name of the person who is bullying you clearly on the paper, with the black pen. Use the name by which they are generally known including their surname if you wish.

Roll the paper up in a tight scroll and tie it securely with the black wool. Say:

I bind you, I bind you
You'll do no harm to me
I bind you, I bind you
I'll do no harm to thee
I bind you, I bind you
Ever more shall be
Blessed Be.

You can simply repeat, 'I bind you from doing harm to me or my friends, for the good of all.' When you have securely tied up the paper with the black thread, tap the thread with your wand. Place the bound scroll at the back of the freezer. Be sure to tell your Mum this is important to you,

so she doesn't pull it out with the fish fingers!
If your Mum won't let you put it in the freezer,
bury it under a stone in the garden. When the
situation is completely resolved, unwrap the scroll
and burn the paper and wool, or bury them deep
in the soil. ✧

INTERVIEW CHARM

If you have an interview for a new school, a part-
time job or a meeting with a teacher, get some
secret support from this interview charm. You'll
need a clear head, the ability to express yourself
pleasantly and some good old-fashioned luck!
Here's how.

You will need
* yellow, green and purple candles
* some yellow tape or ribbon big
  enough to go round your wrist
* three symbols (a horse-shoe, a
  bird and a heart)

NB If you aren't allowed to use candles, get some see-through paper in these colours and shine a torch through them. You can get the symbols from most cake-decorating shops. First light your yellow candle and touch your bird symbol with your wand. Say, 'May my mind be clear as the blue sky.' Then light your green candle and say, 'May people warm to me and like me' as you touch your wand to the heart. Finally light your purple candle, touch your wand to the horse-shoe and say, 'May the Great Mother bring me luck.'

Sew your symbols to your tape while the candles are burning, attaching them as securely as you can. Make sure the tape or ribbon is long enough to tie round your wrist when you go for the interview or meeting (you could hide it under your shirt or jumper so it doesn't show). If you aren't sure about your sewing, bind all three symbols round with the tape and stow this in your pocket or purse. Ready to impress? ✧

TO ACE THAT TEST

The best way to get good marks is to work hard – sad but true! No amount of spells will get you great grades if you've loafed about all year. But a bit of effort, topped up by some magic to keep your mind sharp and clear, should make the grade.

You will need
* a yellow candle
* some lavender oil
* three almonds

Do this spell the evening before the test, after you have finished your revising. If you can have a shower or bath before the spell use lavender soap or bath oil. This helps to cleanse away all the tension, stress and worry.

Light your candle and relax. Take up the lavender oil (remember your allergy testing) and place a little on your tummy saying, 'May the body be strong.' Place a little on your chest and say, 'May the heart be peaceful' and another small dab on your forehead saying, 'May the mind be sharp and clear.'

Tap each of the almonds with your wand and say, 'May I be blessed with wisdom, good memory and good luck.' Then eat the almonds. Dab a little lavender oil on your pillow and sleep soundly before you do your stuff! ✧

MENTAL MARVEL

This spell will help to sharpen your mind. Use it for times when you have to study or be really on the ball.

You will need
* a yellow candle
* a yellow garment or scarf
* a lavender joss stick

Light the yellow candle and say out loud:

Mercury so swift of flight
Make my mind clear and bright.

Light the joss stick from the candle and pass the scarf or garment through the smoke three times. Wear the garment or scarf whenever you need to concentrate or be really perceptive. ✧

YOU'RE A STAR!

Of course you want to be really popular at school, and successful, too! Here's a spell to help you shine and make everyone want to come and be near you.

You will need ✳ a gold star
✳ a cinnamon joss stick

For the star you can use a Christmas decoration or make your own from card and chocolate wrappers.

Light your joss stick and imagine everything negative leaving you. Blow hard if you like, 'seeing' any bad feelings being blown away, like black clouds. Keep blowing till you are sure they are gone.

Hold the star between your hands and imagine yourself being popular and successful. Imagine your day at school with everyone being warm towards you, and you feeling confident and really good about yourself. Imagine things going your way.

Now hold the star above your head. Clearly picture it fixed there, shining out on the world. Now say, 'I'm a star, I'm a star,' as many times as you like.

If you need to repeat this spell, cleanse the star very gently with a little lemon juice dissolved in water. If the star could tarnish don't make it wet all over – this is a symbolic cleansing. Shine on! ✧

CHAPTER SEVEN

Fab families

We all want a peaceful life at home but it isn't always easy. Try out these spells to help you and your family chill out and get along. ✧

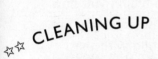CLEANING UP

No, this isn't about tidying your room – although that will help too! This spell is to clear the air if you've had a row, or want to make a new start.

You will need
* a lemon
* a bowl of water
* your wand

When you have the house to yourself, cut the lemon in half and squeeze some of the juice into the bowl of water. Tap it with your wand, imagining that it has a supernatural purifying power. Now just go round the house and, using your fingers, shake a very little of the water around each room. All clear! ✧

✩✩ ANTI-GRUMPS SPELL

We all get the blues sometimes and when you're growing up things can be especially difficult. You're struggling to cope with all the changes in you, and yet older people keep telling you how great you ought to feel! Don't worry if you get depressed – there's nothing wrong with that. Anyway, magical help is on its way!

Chocolate is a cure for the effect of the Dementors in *Harry Potter*. In fact there are substances in chocolate that do make us feel great and have a similar effect on the brain to being in love. No wonder we're all crazy about chocolate!

You can boost its effects by this spell.

You will need
* your wand
* some natural orange food colouring
* a small knife
* a bar of your favourite chocolate

NB For the food colouring substance use turmeric or something similar from your local health food store, or just use fresh orange juice (do not use tartrazine). Sit in gentle sunshine if you can. Make sure that you are peaceful and undisturbed. Don't try to feel anything – just relax. When you are ready make three small holes in the chocolate bar. Into each of the holes drop three drops of the orange juice or food colouring. Tap the bar with your wand and say:

Sunshine, sunshine, enter here
No more sadness, no more tears
The heart be light, the mind be clear
Sunshine, sunshine, bring me cheer.

Visualize the power of the sun entering the chocolate bar. Close your eyes and imagine it shining through, lovely, warm and hearty. Then ... eat the chocolate! ✧

PEACE IN THIS HOUSE

It can be really upsetting if your folks are arguing a lot. Of course it doesn't help when they won't talk it over with you! Here is a very simple spell to bring some peace indoors.

You will need
* a peace lily in a pot
* your wand

A peace lily will cost about £5 and you can probably get one from your local supermarket or garden centre. Choose a plant that has a white flower already growing on it. If you cannot get a peace lily some sprigs of dried lavender will be almost as good.

Sit in the centre of your house if you can, but if not do the spell up in your room. Have the lily or your lavender with you, on your lap and touch

it with your wand. Close your eyes. Imagine there is a gentle, pinkish glow coming from the lily or lavender. You can talk to it if you wish, saying that you know it is a plant of peace, would it please lend its power to your home and help you; in turn you will care for it. Imagine that this lovely glow is slowly spreading all through the house.

When you feel you have visualized all you can, carefully take a little of the pollen from the centre of the lily flower and put just a little in the four corners of your home (do this carefully because the pollen can stain). If you are using lavender, put just a few grains of the dried flower in each corner. Do this downstairs and upstairs if you can.

Have a drink of water to ground yourself after your visualization. Now you have to keep your promise, so if you have a peace lily look after it as best you can. Don't over-water it, follow the instructions on the label, talk to it (yes, plants really DO respond!) and just keep a sensitive eye on it. It won't be the end of the world if it dies, so don't worry! If you have used lavender then sow some lavender seeds outside so that lavender may spread and flourish. Let there be peace! ✧

☆☆ COMMUNICATION SPELL

Why does it sometimes seem as if no-one's listening? Or maybe you just can't get the words out? Perhaps the whole family is having trouble expressing themselves and the air is heavy with repressed feelings. Try this spell to clear the air and start talking.

You will need ✳ one lavender joss stick
✳ your wand

With the joss stick smouldering, go round the house from room to room, making sure the fragrant smoke gets into every corner. Imagine it cleansing anything muddy and negative. Open the windows and doors if you like and 'see' the negativity leaving as grey clouds and the peaceful, clean lavender atmosphere taking over. When you have completed this, go round the house again with your wand. This will be especially good with

a hazel wand. Wave your wand into all the
corners, imagining sparks and colours coming
from it, brightening up the air and making
everything alive and vibrant. It could get noisy –
well, you asked for it! ✧

CHAPTER EIGHT

Potions class

Making magical potions is great for two reasons. Firstly, taking something inside your body that you have magically charged up is a very powerful way of making changes; and secondly, you get to guzzle all the yummy stuff you've used! ✧

☆☆ HOT STUFF POTION

This potion is great if you're going out and wanna knock 'em dead. It'll give you a boost if you're nervous and help you shine. It's good for sport, too.

You will need
* a can of tomato soup, preferably organic
* a pinch of coriander, chilli powder and cardamom
* a saucepan
* a cup or your chalice
* your wand

All these are curry ingredients, but they have a magical va-va-voom. If you are lucky your Mum or Dad will have them in their kitchen cupboard.

Carefully heat the soup and as it begins to simmer add a tiny amount of each of the spices (too much and the taste could be too strong).

Point the tip of your wand at the soup and circle it three times, clockwise, saying:

Here within this magic brew
Energy, strength, attraction, too.

Visualize yourself carrying all before you! If you have decided to use your chalice, let the soup cool before you pour it in, especially if it is glass.

Grated cheese added to this potion calms it down a bit and adds a feeling of safety and security.

Share with a friend if there is some to spare and slurp as much as you like! ✧

☆☆ CHUMMY CHOCOLATE

This is a great cheer-you-up potion, or you can share it with a friend to bring you closer and make you feel really good about each other.

You will need
* ✳ organic hot chocolate powder
* ✳ organic milk
* ✳ organic brown sugar
* ✳ some marshmallows
* ✳ a cocktail stick
* ✳ a whisk
* ✳ a mug
* ✳ a saucepan

Measure out the milk – one cup or two – and pour into a saucepan. Heat it very gently and do not allow it to boil. Following the instructions on the tin, make up the hot chocolate, whisking it and adding sugar to taste.

Keeping the pan of hot chocolate warm, but not boiling, circle your wand clockwise over the pan saying:

Cheery chocolate, warm and sweet
Turn my life into a treat.

Using the cocktail stick, scratch symbols or letters on the marshmallows to signify nice things such as kisses, smiley faces, or 100%. You could even sketch that groovy mini you want to buy. What you draw doesn't have to be clear – you know what you mean!

Pour the chocolate into the mug or mugs and drop the marshmallows in, visualizing the goodies they are bringing. Watch them melt into the creamy drink and sip slowly. Delicious! ✧

☆☆ ROCKET FUEL

This belter of a brew is good enough for Harry
Potter. It is designed to give you the energy and
courage to tackle anything, but it is NOT nice!
You will only need a few drops on your tongue –
more could make you feel sick.

You will need

* five nettle leaves
* spring water
* five fresh basil leaves
* a pinch of ground ginger
* five cumin seeds
* white pepper
* a jar
* your wand

Gather five nettle leaves when the Moon is almost
full. Try to pick them from an unpolluted area.
Please be VERY careful that what you are picking
IS nettle – check first with an adult and don't
under any circumstances take chances. The wrong

 wild plant could be poisonous and make you very ill or even kill you. No respectable and responsible witch gets laid low by her own concoction! Wear gloves, and wash the leaves thoroughly.

Bring half a litre of spring water to the boil and add the nettle leaves, with five fresh basil leaves. (You can get basil plants from most supermarkets.) When these have softened add a pinch of ground ginger, five cumin seeds (a curry ingredient) and some white pepper. Wave your wand over the mixture and dance like a witch-doctor making as much noise as you can. Chant, 'This hour, this hour, the gods give me power.' If Mum isn't keen on you doing voodoo in her kitchen, then wait for the stuff to cool and dance round it in your room.

When your potion has simmered for five minutes, let it cool and strain it into an empty jar (NOT your chalice). If you have too much liquid, pour the excess outside on to the ground, not down the sink. Have just a tiny sip – it will give you all you need. If you seal the jar the potion should keep for a few days in the fridge. ✧

✫☆ FRIENDSHIP POTION

Share this fruity concoction with your friends and you'll all be feeling sweet.

You will need
* one banana
* one orange
* six white grapes
* a handful of mint leaves
* a small glass of apple juice
* your wand
* a blender

Simply put all the fruit and the juice in the blender. Tap it with your wand and whizz up the ingredients. Pour a little into everyone's glass, with just a leaf or two of mint on the top. Sip happily! ✦

☆☆ CLEVER POTION

Try this when you have to revise for exams or study really hard.

You will need
* a sachet of fennel tea
* a little honey
* a yellow mug
* your wand

Make the tea following the instructions on the packet and add a little honey. Tap the mug with your wand and say:

This brew is magic for my mind
Inspiration here I find.

Let the tea cool and sip it. If you don't like the taste you don't have to finish it. ✧

90

☆☆ SLEEP POTION

This is for times when you're stressed out.

You will need
* a sachet of chamomile tea
* some honey
* your chalice

Make the tea in your chalice, following the instructions on the pack. (Be careful if your chalice is glass. Make it first in a mug, let it cool and then transfer, so the glass doesn't break.) Add the honey. Say out loud: 'Great Mother, give me peace and the blessing of sleep.' Sip gently and sweet dreams! ✧

CHAPTER NINE

On the side of the light

In times gone by witches had a very bad time of it. Even today some people say witches are devil-worshippers and evil. However, witches do not believe in the devil, so they certainly do not worship him. And how can it be evil to worship Nature and the Goddess? Most people who criticize witchcraft do not know what it is, and many people are afraid of the unknown and any belief-system that challenges their familiar way of looking at things. It is true that witches do not let anyone tell them what to do; each person makes her or his own contact with the Goddess. There are no gospels or lists of things you should do. There is only that powerful little phrase, 'Harm none'.

Goddess-worship is great for girls because it makes them feel strong and important. It's also great for the environment, because earth is a manifestation of the Goddess, and so receives true respect and caring. It is one thing to be told you should look after the environment, recycle, care for trees and so on – we all know that we like to get out of 'shoulds'! But it's another thing when you feel, deep inside, that you want to care for the earth because it is the Mother Goddess. Then you do it naturally.

So, as a witch, you're definitely one of the good guys! Here are some spells for you to help the world in which we live and the people and animals that it supports. Doing them will make you feel great. ✧

☆☆ LOVE IS ALL AROUND SPELL

In Chapter Two we met the idea of the magic circle (see pages 27–28). Here you are going to use it in a similar way to a fully-fledged adult witch, and send love out into the environment.

Do this spell when you are in a good mood and feel you have some happy vibes to spread. Full Moon is a great time.

You will need
* a white or red candle
* your chalice
* a joss stick
* your wand
* your stone
* a dish of dried rose petals
* some fruit juice
* a treat, such as chocolate

Find out which way your room faces, roughly, and put your stone in the North, candle in the South, chalice in the West and joss stick in the East. Open the door of your room and tell anything negative to get out – flap it away as an imaginary grey mist, with your hands. Keep doing this until you feel it is completely clear.

Stand in the middle with the dish of rose petals at your feet. Face North, point your wand towards the North, and form a circle, clockwise, all around you, with the point of the wand. Imagine light streaming from your wand and condensing as a circle around you. If you live in the Southern Hemisphere it is best to put the stone in the South and the candle in the North, and draw the circle anti-clockwise, because this is the way the Sun moves in the Southern Hemisphere. Also the Element of Earth, which

 your stone represents, is linked to the area of the sky where the Sun and Moon do not appear, hence the placing of the stone in the South.

When your circle is complete, stand facing your stone and ask for the blessing of the Mother Goddess. Dance round your rose petals in the same direction as you made your circle, saying, 'Love is around and within, love is everywhere.' When you feel you have done this enough point your wand at the rose petals and imagine love streaming from your wand into the petals. Do this for as long as you feel comfortable – probably a few seconds.

Put the rose petals by your stone, sit facing it and have your juice and chocolate saying:

I eat and drink in celebration of the Nature Goddess. May I be blessed, may all be blessed.

When you've finished, hold your wand over the stone and imagine your circle being re-absorbed by the wand. Have some more to eat and drink. Spread the rose petals outside and ask that the world be blessed. ✧

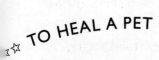

TO HEAL A PET

It's sad to see your pet suffer. Of course sick animals should be taken to the vet, but you can help with this spell.

You will need
* an amber bead
* a holey stone or small piece of clear quartz crystal
* a small green bag
* your pet!

Hold your pet and think loving thoughts – this should not be difficult! If you know where the problem is, rub your bead or stone very gently clockwise (anti-clockwise in the Southern

97

Hemisphere) over the place, imagining warmth and healing entering your pet. Imagine your pet well and happy. Be very careful not to hurt your pet.

Cut a little of your pet's fur and wrap it round the bead or stone and put this in the green bag. If you can't cut your pet's fur you can use a piece of fur from your sofa or your pet's bed. When your pet is better, bury the hair and wash the bead or stone with spring water, imagining it cleansed from within. If your pet isn't furry (e.g. a tortoise or fish) you can use a drawing or photograph instead. ✧

✩✩ TO HEAL WILD ANIMALS

Maybe you are concerned about the dolphins, badgers, red squirrels or other wild animals in the world. It is hard to feel powerless when animals are suffering but with this spell you can do your bit.

You will need
* something to represent the habitat of the animal
* a green candle
* some eucalyptus or lavender oil

To symbolize the habitat, you could use some earth for a badger, water for a dolphin, or a twig for a squirrel or bird. Light your candle before you start. Just trickle a few drops of the oil into the earth or water, or rub it on the twig and say, 'With this gentle, healing oil may peace, love and healing come to [say the name of the animal].' Imagine the habitat being clean, safe and pleasant for the animal and all being as it should. Send your love to the animals. Afterwards put your earth, water or twig outside, in a park or garden, to return them to the Goddess. ✧

☆☆ HEALING A FRIEND

When your friend is ill, especially if it's your best mate, it's the pits! After you've done your cheer-me-up bit by going round with all the latest goss and an armful of magazines, why not send some unseen help as well?

You will need
* a green tissue or hanky
* some eucalyptus oil
* paper and pen
* a green candle
* some green ribbon
* your wand

Light the candle. Write your friend's name on the piece of paper and tap it with your wand. Put a few drops of eucalyptus oil on the tissue and place this over your friend's name, as if you were pulling a green sheet over her. Sit quite still, imagining her totally well, laughing and having a great time.

Roll up the paper with the name and the green tissue or hanky in a scroll and tie it with the green ribbon. Keep it somewhere safe until your friend is well. Then bury or burn the paper and put the rest away for another time. ✧

CHAPTER TEN

Magical future

Magic has always fascinated or scared people, but at the moment there's a real buzz around it due to films like *Harry Potter* and series like *Charmed*. Is this just a phase? Maybe not.

People have always wondered whether the human mind might be capable of more than it seems. Throughout history there have been people who claimed or who were believed to have special powers. The last two or three hundred years have probably been the least magical with the advances of science and logic. People have come to believe that science has all the answers and all that exists can be seen, touched and pulled apart.

But just as it may have begun to seem that everything could be mapped and defined, a new perspective has

started to emerge. Scientists are beginning to say
that the mind does influence reality. This is called
Quantum Physics: the behaviour of sub-atomic
particles is influenced by the observer. Physicists
such as Niels Bohr and James Wheeler
have advanced the 'Copenhagen
interpretation', which states that no
elementary phenomenon is a phenomenon until
it is observed. This comes close to saying that the
mind influences reality, or certainly is involved
in 'reality'.

So what is reality? Maybe our minds really are
involved in what happens – maybe we are creating
reality, to some extent. After all, physicists tell us
that everything is energy. When we look at a
table, that 'solid' object is a mass of teeming bits
of energy. It is just our brains that interpret it as
a table.

Ancient peoples may well have understood
that the world is energy and that our minds take
part in it. It is possible that there were schools of
magic in Ancient Egypt. Certainly
there were mystery cults, such as that
of Eleusis in Ancient Greece.

Some people believe that humans are evolving, so that we will become more psychic; others that we have lost our psychic powers as we have become more civilized. Maybe the truth is that we are going to regain our psychic powers with a new understanding, as we take on board a new view of reality. ✧

Magical you

If you are interested in magic it is probable that you are interested in expanding your awareness and exploring just what you are capable of. It is possible that in the future there will be a college of magic – what an exciting thought! In the meantime, all you can do is develop your own mind.

Always be sensible about magic and remember that a good witch is also a practical person, who looks after herself and does her best to be healthy and safe – because that way she knows she's more powerful. Magic should be kept in perspective – it isn't going to help to get all spaced out. Always make sure that you back up your spells with action in the outside world and that you hang on to your common sense.

It's easy to make fun of spells and some people may laugh at you – so why tell them? Don't use your 'witchiness' to get attention, or you could get the wrong attention. It is best to keep your interests to yourself, apart from a good friend or two that you can really trust. The most important thing about your magic is that it should make you a stronger, deeper and more powerful person. When you feel right inside then everything falls into place.

Here's a final spell for you to find your power-symbol. You can bear this symbol in mind whenever you need to feel strengthened and protected. You can draw it on a card, or, depending on what it is, you may find it as jewellery. This symbol is special to YOU and you should never tell anyone about it – not even your best friend. ✧

POWER-SYMBOL SPELL

Make sure you really are in the right mood for this spell. You need to be relaxed and peaceful. If you feel impatient or upset, do it another time.

You will need
- ✳ a glass bowl full of water
- ✳ your wand
- ✳ a cinnamon or honeysuckle joss stick
- ✳ a white candle

Light your candle – this spell is best done at night-time, simply by the light of one candle. (If you are not allowed to use candles, do it by a low light, or moonlight.) Light the joss stick. Sit with the bowl on your lap or between your knees. When you feel peaceful and ready, tap the centre of the water with your wand, so that the ripples flow outwards.

Look into the bowl of water, but do not look at the surface. Look right through it and focus your eyes as if they are looking at something very distant. Say, 'Great Mother, show me my power-symbol.'

You may now find that an image or several images form in the water. Or maybe you will see nothing, but find that you are thinking of something or seeing something with your mind's eye. Either way, this is important. Relax and take note.

When you have done this for as long as is comfortable (five minutes is quite enough) then stop gazing and make a note of the impressions you have gained. The chances are you will have seen your power-symbol – you will know it,

 because it will make you feel good. Animals very often appear as power-symbols and they are very strong and helpful. You may also strongly smell or hear something, which will give you a clue to your power-symbol.

Ground yourself by placing your palms to the ground or on your stone. Pour away the water. If you can get a badge or jewellery to represent your power-symbol, then that's great. Remember or wear it whenever you have to face some sort of challenge. It will be your champion. ✧

APPENDIX

Making your own spells

Making your own spells is easy. You will have seen that certain substances are linked to certain purposes, e.g. rose with love, yellow with an active mind and so on. Once you get the hang of what goes with what you can make your own spells.

Magical things are grouped under planets and the Sun and Moon – this has been the case for many hundreds of years. It makes things simpler. Of course, making up your own spells is a matter of confidence and intuition. Only do it if you feel ready. The following list will help. You can find most of these things in New Age shops, and the herbs from the local supermarket or garden centre. ✧

Sun ★★

* confidence, creativity, popularity, success.
* orange (colour and fruit) gold, amber, carnelian, topaz, cinnamon, bay, carnation, frankincense, rosemary, St John's Wort.

Moon ★★

* dreams, healing, psychism, sympathy, family and friendship bonds, intuition.
* white and silver (colour and substance), crystal, moonstone, sapphire, lemon, lemon balm, jasmine, eucalyptus, gardenia, willow.

Mercury ★★

* communication, mentality, thought, study, quick mind.
* yellow, agate, aventurine, mottled jasper, lavender, fennel, almond, mace, mint, peppermint.

Venus ★★

* love, beauty, harmony, friendship, happiness, money (although money can involve the Sun, Jupiter and Saturn too).
* pink and blue, also green, copper, lapis lazuli, jade, coral, emerald, malachite, rose, apple, banana, cardamom, strawberry, thyme, vanilla.

Mars ★★

* energy, courage, fighting spirit.
* red, iron, bloodstone, red jasper, ruby, basil, nettle, carrot, garlic, ginger, pepper.

Jupiter ★★

* good fortune, power, meditation, growth and expansion.
* purple and magenta, tin, amethyst, lepidolite, honeysuckle, sage, clove, nutmeg, dandelion.

Saturn ★★

* binding, ending, grounding, practicality, boundaries, time, letting go.
* black, dark brown, lead, coal, jet, onyx, obsidian, apache tear, comfrey, cypress, patchouli.

Now try out your spell-making abilities and see how you get on with the following exercise. ✧

Exercise

This exercise is designed to test your developing witch powers. If you've read through the book you won't find it hard. Good luck!

a) Put together a charm to make you psychic.

b) Do a spell to help mend a broken heart at the end of a relationship.

c) Make a charm for courage to face an awkward situation.

Now check your spells against the answers over the page. How did you do?

Answers ★★

a) The moon rules psychic stuff. So if you put
   together a spell using moon substances then
   well done. Here is a detailed suggestion. Using
   dried jasmine, white candles, a Moon picture or
   symbol and a clear crystal and jasmine joss
   stick, make a charm similar to the Rose Quartz
   Charm in Chapter Three (see pages 29–31).

b) This is more complicated. Full marks if you
   combined Saturn for ending and Moon for
   healing in any way. Here is a full story. Use a
   black candle (Saturn) for ending and a
   eucalyptus joss stick (Moon) for healing. Cut a
   piece of cord in two, wrap one end round a
   piece of onyx and bury the other. Get the idea?

c) Mars is your mate here so well done if you
   spotted that. This is one way to combine Mars
   ingredients. Why not light a red candle, charge
   up some ginger root with your wand, pop it in
   a red pouch and carry it with you? You've got
   the power!

Index